INSIDER'S SECRETS TO WRITING A LEAD GENERATION BOOK IN 7 DAYS OR LESS

An Easy Cure for Writer's Block for Service Providers and Entrepreneurs

DARCY JUAREZ

ISBN-13: 978-1986567459
ISBN-10: 1986567451

DOWNLOAD THE AUDIOBOOK AND TOOLKIT (INCLUDING ALL THE WORKSHEETS) FOR FREE!

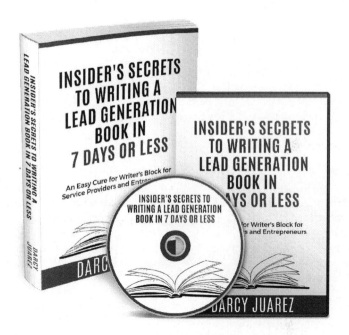

READ THIS FIRST

Just to say thanks for reading my book, I would like to give you the audiobook version PLUS the accompanying toolkit (which includes all the templates and worksheets) absolutely FREE.

Go to www.DarcyJuarez.com/freeaudiobook

TABLE OF CONTENTS

SECTION 1: Can You Really Write a Book?

SECTION 2: Creating Your Book FAST

SECTION 3: Printing and Publishing Your Book

CHAPTER 1

SHOULD YOU WRITE A BOOK?

Have you ever wondered why everyone gravitates towards the author of a book?

Have you ever found yourself gravitating to those who have written the book? Wanting to take their advice, follow their direction, even hire them to solve your problems?

How many times have you heard someone say they choose a provider because he or she "wrote the book"?

Imagine what it would be like to tell your

prospects, *"I'll send you a copy of my book."*

Imagine what it would be like when your clients, your family, your friends say, *"You should read this book."*

How much persuasion and influence will be happening behind the scenes and subconsciously positioning you as the expert in their minds?

If you are looking for the one thing that will finally separate yourself from the competition – there is only one thing that I know of that works overnight. And that is to become an author yourself.

Why?

Because a book is still the number one indicator of an authority figure. When we are seeking out someone to help us solve our problems, whether that is a plumber, a financial planner, a local marketing agency, or coach/consultant or mentor, we are all looking for an authority figure who can quickly solve our biggest problems.

If you are an entrepreneur or small business owner – you NEED a book – BUT it's not the type of book you're likely thinking of.

As an entrepreneur or small business owner, what you really need is a Lead Generation Book which is completely different than most books that you have read.

Maybe you have tried writing a book before…

Maybe you have thought to yourself …

- I would like to write a book, but I don't have time.
- I'd like to write a book, but I heard it costs $30,000+ to write a book.
- I'd like to write a book – but I don't know where to start.
- I'd like to write a book, but what would I ever say.
- I'd like to write a book, but who would listen to me?
- I'd like to write a book, but I am a horrible writer.

What if I told you, I had figured out a way to write a book without actually having to write it?

What if I told you that you could write this book all based on what you already know?

What if I told you that today is the day that your dream of writing your book is about to become a reality.

You're about to discover the process that my students have quietly been using for the last 5 years to quickly and easily write their own lead generation books. In fact, one of my first students went on to write 9 more books using this method over the next 12 months!

These books have;

- Given small business owners and entrepreneurs a platform to share their knowledge and change lives

- Created hundreds of thousands (if not millions) of dollars' worth of business for hundreds of business owners

- Created millions of leads for businesses of every sort

- Landed consulting contracts

- Converted prospects into coaching clients

- Led to speaking opportunities

- Created PR and free exposure

- But most importantly positioned the author as the expert and authority figure they truly are!

If you are a service provider, a coach, a consultant, a speaker, an entrepreneur or small business owner who has a solution to a problem that your prospects desire – this book is for you!

What is a Lead Generation Book?

One of the biggest obstacles that holds so

many people back from writing their book is their belief that they are writing a New York Times bestseller.

You have a HUGE benefit that the New York Times bestsellers don't have – you have a business. They think that writing their book will create a business. You have a completely different goal than they do.

Think about that for a moment.

Their goal is to write a book that will launch their business, launch their career, that will create enough money for their survival. You already have that.

Your goal is to share your knowledge and expertise with as many ideal prospects as you possibly can and a book is one of the vehicles you can use. It also happens to be one of the fastest vehicles.

In reality, you don't want a 300-page book, you don't need 85 edit revisions and years of research. You just need a vehicle to share your story and reach your prospects.

Your prospects is key – your book is not for everyone – it's only for those that you designate as your ideal prospects. You get to write directly to them, as if they were sitting in front of you today and you were just chitchatting. Your book is all about what they want to learn from you.

And my favorite saying, Version 1 is better than Version none. You can continue to release new versions of your book as often as you would like; you are not tied to what you write today.

Our goal with a lead generation book is not to become a bestseller (although there are ways to do that should you want.) Our goal is for this book to provide you with more leads, more clients and ultimately more money for your business.

Why Should You Write a Book?

If you have wisdom, knowledge and expertise that helps your clients better their lives, then you owe it to the world to share your knowledge, and your book can do this.

If this describes you – you're in the right place – I'm about to show you how you can write your own book in as little as one week!

I'm giving you my step-by-step process – the same one that I teach in a 2-day book writing intensive for $5,000 with GKIC (gkic.com); it's the exact process that so many have used to create their own lead generation books.

I've tested this and tweaked it over the last 5 years – teaching it first to the GKIC Peak Performers and then as a part of the Ultimate Lead Generation Machine, a must-have training for all small business owners (www.gkic.com/ultimate-marketing-machine)

So why would I share this, if it's really worth $5,000 to $10,000? Because the act of having the information and sharing knowledge does not reduce the amount of business, clients or customers who want to work with you, but instead increases them. Which also will happen for you.

Let's get started...

This process is broken down into 3 parts

- Can you really write a book in as little as one week?

- How to create your book FAST

- How to publish and print your book for as little as $2.50

CHAPTER 2

WHY DO I NEED A LEAD GENERATION BOOK?

There are 3 big reasons to have a book. The first is for the positing that having a book provides. For the ability to use "author of…" in your introductions, on your website, in your marketing, and in conversations with prospective clients.

If you are like most entrepreneurs I know, you have heard that having a book is the best positioning tool you can own. You know you should have a book, but the thought of writing a book scares you and you have avoided it like the plague.

If you're a coach or consultant (or want to be one) there is no question that you have to have a lead generation book.

If you are currently speaking or plan to speak in front of audiences who aren't familiar with you, you have to have a lead generation book.

A lead generation book is the one tool that every toolbox needs. From Dr. Bill Dorfman to Suze Orman to Dr. Oz it's the one tool that (regardless of how you feel about them professionally) has helped build their business, earn respect and become instant celebrities.

Books hold a unique status in our society – they are a symbol that the author knows what they are talking about (and it's easy – when reading the book to see that they do indeed have unique knowledge.)

The second big reason is that a book creates

price elasticity for your business. The amount that people are willing to pay the "expert" (as defined by having written the book) is significantly higher than the amount they are willing to pay others.

And finally, a book specifically a lead generation book - provides you with a specific marketing tool that has been proven over and over again to out convert competing white papers, ebooks, and free reports that most of your competitors are offering. That's not to say that you don't need or won't use those tools – in fact, a free report is the second marketing asset that every business needs to have (but that's for another book and another story.)

But let's not leave out how proud your mom and dad will be when they get to say, *"My son is the author of _____."* How in awe your friends will be, and your spouse might even think you're cool for a day to two ☺.

As I mentioned before, our goal for writing a lead generation book is completely different than the goal of most who set out to write a book. But we still need to know our goal.

What is the specific result or results that you want from your book?

- **Position yourself as the expert in your field:** This is the best reason (in my mind) to write your lead generation book. You have specific know-how, knowledge, experience, and insight that your prospects and clients can benefit from. You are doing them a disservice by keeping that knowledge locked in your head. With this process, it's easy to create multiple books – only magnifying your position as an expert.

- **Create a name for yourself:** Books have been known to turn household names into celebrities. The best part of working with lead generation books is that you only need to be a celebrity to your target market (not to the entire world.) You can become *THE* chiropractor, dentist, financial planner, real estate agent, mortgage broker, etc. in Canton, Ohio.

- **Drive leads to your business:** A book written to a specific target of people, talking directly to them, providing the information that they are seeking is a marketing asset that can draw attention to you and your business 24/7.

- **Answer the most common questions you receive:** This is a book that is comprised of the most commonly asked questions. If you find yourself constantly answering the same questions, you might find putting those questions into a book that will be used AFTER a client starts working with you, will work for you. Along the lines of *What to expect after surgery.*

- **To gain speaking engagements:** Most people who book speakers (from local chamber events up to keynote events) are looking for social proof that the person that they are hiring has something unique and is qualified to share with their audience. A book is a great way to showcase that and can open many doors for you.

- **Share your unique process for something:**

If what you do is complicated or involves a lot of steps or time, a book is a great way to share the full picture. When you are first meeting with a prospective client, they may not be willing to give you 2 hours to explain what you do and why you do it – but they are willing to read your book! Think about all the things that you don't know about dentistry – that your dentist could provide for you in a book format.

You could learn about the history of X-rays and why they are so safe today. Or from a prospective real estate agent, you could learn about how the home buying process really works.

- **Preheat prospective clients to choose your services over your competitors:** Similar to sharing your unique process, books allow your prospective clients to learn about you, your services and most importantly enlighten them to what you do that your competitors don't (or won't do) in a safe environment. They can take their time, digesting the information and are not feeling rushed or pressured. The ideas are being conveyed without you 'bragging' or 'selling' them. Your book creates a safe, contained environment for prospects to choose you.

- **Convert prospects to clients:** Your book can be a great tool to provide prospects who are on the fence and ready to move forward.

Ultimately, the determining factor of success is completely up to you. Knowing what you want to accomplish helps you from getting bogged down by trying to be everything to everyone.

Can I Really Write a Book?

Once you know your end goal, writing the book becomes much easier. After all, you already possess the wisdom and the expertise (the only problem is it's currently trapped in your head) and until now, there hasn't been a great way to get that expertise out of your head and onto the paper.

The process we are going to go through

today involves very little 'writing' and to a degree very little thinking. You already know everything you need to write a book. You have been living this for years in your business, but your prospects don't know this.

Think about the last time you tried something new, the last time you set out to buy something – you had very little information. You were looking for someone who could guide you, who could help you sort through the mounds of information that was available...

- The first time you decided that you should have a professional manage your money
- The last time you went to buy or sell your home
- The last time you went to buy a car
- The last time you had to find a specialist
- The last time you wanted to solve that nagging back pain

Let's take that nagging back pain as an example. You probably aren't excited to call 5 different chiropractors, schedule appointments, show up for the appointment and listen through their explanation. How great would it have been if one of those chiropractors instead of pushing to schedule an appointment gave you their book?

You could sit at home with a cup of coffee and peruse through the book at your own pace. You could get a feeling for who the doctor was, how he treated back pain, and how you're treatment would work.

Now, when you make that appointment, your excited, you feel like you already know the doctor and you're ready to get started.

Now, think about it from the doctor's side. She just gained a patient who is excited and ready to move forward quickly (and likely with little resistance) from a marketing asset that was working behind the scenes for her. She spent time writing her book, and her book worked to convert the patient.

That's what this is all about!

Keys to your success with this process

1. **Embrace the process** – What we are about to go through may seem silly at times, or like we are moving too slow, but I promise you, this process does work. Every time I teach this process to a live workshop, I explain this at the beginning and there is always the one person who doesn't do the work at the beginning of the day, who ultimately regrets it at the end of the day when everyone else has started flying through their books. I promise the work you put in at the beginning will pay off in the end.

2. **Take action** – nothing will happen until you start. I promise that you can write a book in 7 days or less, but that won't happen if you don't take action.

3. **Commit to the process** – The worst thing you can do is to keep starting and then stopping because you are looking for a different way to do it. Commit to this process and you will have a completed book.

4. **Version 1 is better than Version none** – The best thing about this process is that your book doesn't ever have to be finished. You can keep making revisions, you can

change every page of the book, if you'd like. But it can't accomplish your goals if it's never actually put out into the world. We will put "Version 1" on this one, we will launch it, and then you can go back and create Versions 2, 3, 4, 5 (or you can just write Books 2, 3, 4 and 5)

Now that you agree that you NEED a book, you're likely wondering what you should write about. In the next chapter, I'll break down how to think about your 'content' as it relates to your business and your book.

CHAPTER 3

I HAVE NO IDEA WHAT I SHOULD WRITE ABOUT

The goal of your book is to introduce prospective clients to you and your business. This is your chance for them to get to know you – for you to WOW them with your expertise, knowledge and showcase the success that you have had.

Your book is all about helping your prospect and should be written as if you are talking directly to them.

23

You want to be talking to their biggest fears and their biggest objections and overcoming both in your book.

You want to be thinking about what your prospect needs to know to move forward. How can you make them feel comfortable in choosing you and your products or services.

I think it's easiest when you start thinking of what you would currently say to prospective clients – what questions do they ask you? What stories do you tell them to help them understand what you do? What statistics do you show them? What client success stories do you share?

If you had all the time in the world to describe to a prospective client what your business is about, why you started doing what you are doing, how many people you have helped, how you have changed lives, how you have protected clients through your work... If you could say anything to showcase your work, what would it be?

The reason a lead generation book can be

so easy to write is that everything you need for your book is already in your head. And the reason that your lead generation book can be so difficult to write is because it's all in your head ☺

The goal of this book, and what I do, is to try and help you quickly and easily take everything that is in your head and get that out onto paper so that you can share your gifts with the world. So that you can help more people through the work you do.

After all, don't we owe it to people to share our gifts? Couldn't we help so many more people if they just knew more about us?

How To Choose Your Book Type

There are a few themes that you might want to consider for your book:

1. **Top 10 questions:** This is where I usually suggest that most people start. It only requires you to start thinking through the common questions that you are asked or that you think that prospects should know

about you, your business or your services. This book type works best for the small business owner who may or may not be selling services. You will see how this process works very well for this type of book.

2. **Your unique process:** I like this type of book for information marketing business, coaches, and consultants. This book type has you talking through and explaining your process for what you do.

   If you are a life coach, you are walking people through your 5-step process for bettering their life. If you are a marketing consultant, you're explaining your 7-step processes for flooding a business with new clients.

3. **How we do x, y, z:** I like this type of book for service-based businesses, like financial planning. For businesses where people are easily overwhelmed by the intricacies and nuances that make you successful.

   This type of book gives you the platform to

really showcase your knowledge.

Most people are afraid if they teach people how to do what they do, that they won't hire them. Except the opposite proves to be true. The more that you can explain exactly what you do, the more comfortable people are in having you do it for them. This type of books works great if you do the services for your clients.

Section 2

Creating Your Book Fast

CHAPTER 4

HOW DO I GET THE EXPERTISE OUT OF MY HEAD AND ONTO THE PAPER?

What I love about this process is it's something that once learned you can do over and over again to create as many books as you would like.

I believe that the current record is held by Paul Hogan and his daughter, Katie Hogan, who were in the first ever class I taught this to and used this method to write 10 more books!

Here is Paul Hogan with all 10 of the books he wrote after learning this process.

Most people get caught up in their own minds, their own self-doubts and really get in their own way. Most spend so much time worried about what others will think, worried that they don't actually have anything to say that anyone will want to read.

What if I told you that most people will never actually read your book? Would that help you overcome your fear of putting yourself out there? That was the little push that Paul Hogan needed to put himself out there – and once he did, he became unstoppable!

Now, I am not saying that your book shouldn't be good. I have to assume that you do have something good to say and something that will help others (this is the premise that we will move forward with.)

What I am saying is that the purpose of a lead generation book is not necessarily to be read cover to cover – but instead to showcase your knowledge and expertise and then for those that choose to read the entire book for it to be worth their time.

Many people think that if a book is written in just 7 days, that we must not be writing very good books. And that is far from the truth.

I remember, when I was in college, watching as so many students would complain about how they never had enough time to finish their projects. And I would think – they have to be crazy. They have class for maybe 4 hours a day, that's it, the rest of the time is free and they can't finish on time?

Yet, somehow I managed to finish those same projects on time with the same 4 hours of class, but I also added 3 hours of practice (I played collegiate volleyball), 1 hour of weight-lifting, not to mention all the traveling.

I come to find out that there's a real explanation for that – it's called Parkinson's law. Which states that work will expand to fill the time available for its completion.

It also explains why we can finish so much when we are under tight deadlines. So we don't really need months and months on end to accomplish this; we just need to give ourselves the deadline of 7 days (or a weekend) and we can make it happen!

A shorter amount of time means more focused time spent on completing your goal. More focused time + System for speed = Book written.

How to Move Quickly Through the Process

We can move quickly through writing the book, because the entire book is based on the information that you already know – the information that you recite every day to your prospects and customers. It's your expertise and what makes you unique, special, and such an asset to your clients. Because of this, there is no time needed for research or data gathering and we can move quickly.

As experts in our fields, there is no way you can ever impart all of your wisdom to a new client. So you have likely gotten good at creating a short and concise description of what you do, but there are always pieces of the puzzle that your clients (even your long-time clients) didn't know you know or didn't know you provide.

Let's take, for instance, a financial planner. While you might have a pamphlet that provides your background, your education, any designations you might have, there is no time for you to really explain your

35

philosophies on money, how money moves, how money grows, what exactly a financial planner does for their clients, everything that the public needs to know about saving for retirement, the mistakes that people make when creating financial plans, how insurance fits into the picture, scenarios that might arise when planning for retirement, the best ways to fund college educations, etc.

Yet, if I got you going in conversation, you would likely have a lot to say about each of those topics and probably hundreds more.

Your book is your opportunity to shine, your opportunity to showcase all the knowledge and expertise that you have. And when someone reads that book and tries to compare you to another financial planner, it will be very difficult to not choose you!

For most, the fear and panic sets in when they are faced with a blank piece of paper or a blank computer screen and told to *write*. We all panic, freeze up and instantly find that we have writer's block.

How to Eliminate Writer's Block

I want to eliminate the writer's block and have you producing your book in record time. In the title I say 7 days and that is more than doable if you will commit to the process and dedicate the time to actually implementing. I have seen plenty who complete this in a weekend.

Business owners rarely have time to write a 300-page book and, honestly, no one wants to read a 300-page book – that takes time to read, and we are all short on time in our days.

People are looking for concise information that will answer their most pressing questions. I have found that 80-100 pages makes a great lead generation book.

Of course, yours can be shorter or longer, it all depends on what you have to say.

Read that line again – *that will answer their most pressing questions.* This is why this system is set up to have you answer questions rather than creating complicated outlines or trying to write from a blank piece of paper.

Wait... I Don't Have to Write the Book ☺

Instead of thinking of this as *writing* your book, think of this as *answering the most pressing questions* but instead of having to do that over and over again with every prospect, customer or client you can leverage your time and efforts to create your book and then let your book work for you for the next 2-5-10 years!

You put in 7 days today and you can have a book that works for you, attracts new prospects, creates clients, and has people talking about you for 7 years to come.

Instead of writing, you're going to be *talking* through your book. All you need is a way to record yourself. Which is as easy as an app on your phone, a voice recorder, or using a free conference line from your computer. You can really do this from anywhere!

Why do I like to have you talk out your

book? Because talking is the natural way that we communicate ideas and information. Writing is actually not the natural way we communicate. So trying to learn how to write a book is like trying to learn how to swim while going upstream. It's just not as natural and easy going as it could be.

Plus, when we talk through our book, our readers feel like we are talking to them and not at them. It feels conversational (because that is how it started) and to the reader it feels like you are in the room talking to them instead of at them (as tends to come across in conventional books.)

They get a chance to know you and bond with you through your words – and we know that people choose to do business with people they know, like and trust. You don't want your book to be cold and lacking any feeling or emotions (that come out naturally when we are talking.)

When people understand your processes, the whys behind what you do, how you got to where you are, and who you are as a person, they are more inclined to move forward with you quicker.

Before we get started, let me give you 3 keys to successfully writing your book,

1. **Version 1 is better than Version none.** Get the book out there as quickly as you can it can't be making you money while sitting on your desk (which is what I say about a lot of things ☺.) You can always update your book, add to it, remove things, etc. at any time – that's the wonderful thing about self-publishing, is that you can make changes at any time.

   You may not take it to the extremes I do, but I will release a book before even having an editor review for grammar and punctuation. I will release the book before I am in love with the cover graphics.

   I subscribe to what we call the MVP (minimally viable product). Meaning that I have self-edited the book (read through it twice myself, maybe had a second set of eyes go through it.) With one of the books I wrote, we had it out there for 6 months – driving people to a high end coaching program – before we hired an editor and fixed all the grammatical errors and republished the book.

The key is to detach yourself emotionally from "needing to be perfect" and focus your time and energy on the bigger picture things that will move the needle for your business. We will never be perfect – there will always be someone who is jealous of your success and nit-picks at the little things that don't matter in the big picture.

2. **Embrace the process.** Trust me, I know, I watch people fight this in every class I teach. They want to shortcut the process outlined in the next chapter – and they come to regret it further down the road. I am about to walk you through a brainstorming process and create a way for you to easily add to your

brainstorming, a way for you to easily move the pieces around until they fit the way you want to all without losing any pieces. It may seem silly or unnecessary in the beginning, but I promise you will use all the pieces, and I promise that you will start to fly through the actual *writing* of your book.

3. **Take action.** I can't stress this enough – nothing happens by osmosis. The difference between an ordinary business and extraordinary business is implementation!

Let's get started. You will want to grab a pack of index cards, many like the colored ones, but you can use any index cards you can find.

CHAPTER 5

THE BRAINSTORM...

Okay. Now it's time to get into the meat of this process. This process is all about brainstorming – there are no right answers or wrong answers – our goal is simply to get as much information as we can down so that we can go back through and tighten it up and create a flow.

For some, you may find that starting with a mind-map helps your brain spit out what's locked inside. Before you jump to the index cards.

For example, when I started writing this book – I was on an airplane and didn't have my index cards with me, so I started with a sheet of paper …

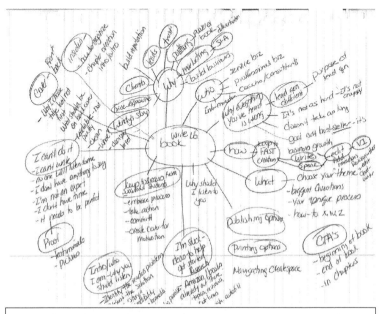

This was my first brainstorm for this book. While I was on an airplane, I just started jotting down everything I could think of related to the topic. And before I knew it, my brain had spurted out over 16 chapters of content.

For most, you can bypass this brainstorming step and start by grabbing a stack of your index cards - start with at least 10 - and I want you to just brainstorm as many big questions, keys to your process, challenges, ideas, objections you hear, stories you can tell, points you want to make, everything and anything you can think of. The more of these that you can phrase as the questions that someone would ask you, the better.

You want to put your thought down as a question on your index card. The reason we do it this way is because in the end you will have someone interviewing you to extract this information from your head and the better worded your question is, the more natural your response and, therefore, your writing will be.

For instance, I have a card that reads *"Why do you need a book?"* The better way to word that card is *"Why does someone need a book?"* It's only slightly different, but it will mean the world to you when you are asking yourself the question and the answers will flow.

Here's what that looked like for this book – you will notice that they are in no particular order, they are just questions and thoughts that I hear when talking to people about writing their books.

To help your brain, let's take a look at some examples in other businesses…

Brainstorming Examples:

For a marketing business
- How do I get new clients?
- What affects local SEO?
- What do I need to do first?
- How do I know if it's working?

For a Dentist:
- Do I really need to see the dentist 2x a year?
- How do I prevent cavities?
- Do I really need fluoride?

For a Real Estate Agent:
- What do I need to know as a first-time home buyer?
- What has changed in real estate in the last 10 years?

For a Lawyer:
- What do I do if I am in a car accident?
- What are the fees?

For a Business Coach:
- Why everything you've heard about building a business is wrong
- Why is using a coach important?
- Isn't it expensive?
- What is your process for building a business?
- What do I need to do first?
- How do I get business FAST?
- Why is it so hard to run a business?

Generic questions everyone can use:
- Why should you care about _____?

- What is the cost of not doing ____?
- What are the costs associated with ____?
- What do I need to do first?

If you are ready to go, the ideas are flying, skip the next few chapters, and go straight to page 55. If you're still drawing a blank and want a few ideas on how to jump start your creative process, continue through the next few pages.

I'm Still Drawing a Blank

Here are a couple more things I suggest if you need to jump-start your brainstorming...

1. **Search Amazon** for books that are already written on your topic. We don't actually care how many books are already out there because our goal is not to compete and sell on Amazon; our goal is to use our book for our own lead generation marketing. But we can scrape a lot of good information from what has already been written.

   a. **Topics.** Search by your topic and see what other titles are out there.

The Chiropractic Evolution: Health From the Inside Out Sep 14, 2011
by Moore, D.C., David R.

Paperback
$14.99 *Prime*
Get it by Saturday, Jan 21

More Buying Choices
$11.75 used & new (30 offers)

Kindle Edition
$8.99
Auto-delivered wirelessly

★★★★☆ · 7
Trade in yours for an Amazon Gift Card up to $1.80

Renegade Lawyer Marketing: How Today's Solo and Small-Firm Lawyers Survive and Thrive in a World of Marketing...
Aug 27, 2015
by Ben Glass

Kindle Edition
$9.99
Auto-delivered wirelessly

★★★★★ · 5

Great Legal Marketing: How Smart Lawyers Think, Behave and Market to Get More Clients, Make More Money, and Still
Get Home in Time for Dinner Mar 1, 2012
by Benjamin W Glass

Paperback
$17.95 *Prime*
Only 17 left in stock - order soon.

More Buying Choices
$9.77 used & new (57 offers)

Kindle Edition
$7.99
Auto-delivered wirelessly

★★★★☆ · 28

Five Deadly Sins That Can Wreck Your Injury Claim May 1, 2008
by Ben Glass

Paperback
$19.95 *Prime* | FREE One-Day
FREE One-Day Delivery on qualifying orders over $35
Only 1 left in stock - order soon.

More Buying Choices
$10.00 used & new (11 offers)

7 Highly Effective Steps To Get The Money You Deserve: When You've Been Injured In A Kansas Car Accident (7 Highly
Effective Ways To Get The Money You Deserve Book 1) Dec 22, 2013
by Paul Hogan

Kindle Edition
$0.00 kindleunlimited
Read this and over 1 million books with Kindle Unlimited.

$0.99 to buy
Auto-delivered wirelessly

b. **Table of Contents.** Take a look at the table of contents for books in your subject matter to see what others are writing about – this can help you if you think you are missing something.

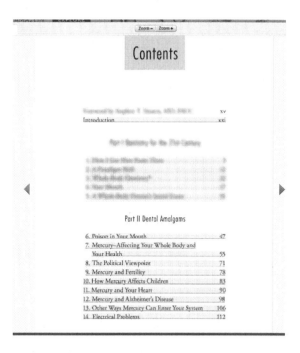

Contents

c. **Reviews.** Look through the reviews for the books. I actually care more about the bad reviews than I do the good ones. Reviews can tell you what readers were looking for from that title, what was missing in the book, or what they were expecting. All of these can be good things for you to include in your book. This is an especially good tip if you are providing a service that is widely searched for – like marketing services vs. a service provider, like a dentist.

Top Customer Reviews

★★★☆☆ **Great book for general information, but not hard specifics.**
By A Customer on February 4, 1999

Format: Paperback

I will be buying a house in about 8-10 months and want to make sure I dont make an expensive mistake. I've read this whole book since I got it from Amazon, and overall I'm glad I read it, but wish I had checked it out of the library instead. It's an EXCELLENT book for generals - general facts, general information, to be pointed in the right general direction. But it's not a good book for cold hard facts and really valuable specifics. It wont turn you into a real negotiating shark or wheeler and dealer when you're dealing with agents or mortgage brokers (which is the kind of information I was looking for).

This book is very slanted towards New York and Chicago, also, because that is where the author's experience lies. But I'm in North Carolina, and some of the information presented as gosepl in this book is just plain factually incorrect for my state. This can be really misleading and problematic depending on your state if you try to follow this book too closely.

The book does contain great reference sections on contracts, resources, and real estate terms; and it also has mortgage payment tables in the back (but they only go up to 100,000 and who really spends less than 100K anymore?).

Although I have said more negative and positive, this is a nice book in a lot of ways. If you know nothing about what is involved in buying a house, definitely get this book. It's wonderful for basic introductory information and it is a pretty hefty book (450 pgs - great value for the cover price). But if you know what is involved and are looking for "inside" information and consumer protection advice on negotiations with brokers, agents, lawyers, mortgage brokers, title companies, etc etc., get something else. If you really want to know about tricks and traps and shady dealings to avoid, you wont find much of that in this book. It's a real estate primer and a wonderful read - but very basic, simple information.

> This review tells me that there weren't enough examples that this reader could use and what they were looking for. The second thing it tells me is that this topic could be segmented into different parts of the country or large urban areas vs. suburban areas (which gives me 2 potential books I can write – or topics I can address in my book. It tells me the reader believes, these to be different – whether they are or not is irrelevant.

★★★☆☆ **It's a bit dated**
By Nano on November 24, 2014

Format: Paperback | Verified Purchase

This book should have been upgraded. It's out of date, written before 2008 when many houses lost value. I'll still read it, but Ms. Glink needs to revise it quite a bit. Not sure how useful it will be- maybe the 100 questions stay the same from year to year.

> Comment | One person found this helpful. Was this review helpful to you? Yes | No | Report abuse

> This review gave me the idea of having a big idea card on "what has changed in the last x years in this industry" – the perception that things are out of date is always high. And talking about what has changed allows you to bring something new to the conversation.

2. **Use auto-fill** in Google to tell you what people are searching for.

This gives me the idea that I should address price, expected prices, and why prices are what they are so that my readers aren't feeling like they are "ripped off."

This gives me ideas for multiple cards if I am a dentist...

- How do I understand dental insurance?
- How does dental insurance work?
- What are the costs associated with dental insurance for the patient and the doctor?
- What does dental insurance cover – what doesn't it cover and why?
- Does dental insurance cover braces?

3. **Forums** are still a great place to read what others are thinking – from behind a

computer screen they will tell you exactly how they feel. You will have to take things with a grain of salt, but you can learn a lot about how people are thinking and feeling about your industry; what they like, what they don't like, who they trust, who they don't trust, etc.

4. **Facebook Groups**. The newest version of a forum is found in Facebook groups. You want to be a part of these in your industry so that you can see in real time what's affecting your potential customers.

Okay. Enough "research." I told you you wouldn't have to do that, and I only suggest you spend a few minutes if you need to jump-start your brainstorming...

Let's Get To Work ...

If you haven't already, pull out a set of index cards (10-20 to start.) Put 1 big idea, thought, or question down per card.

Set a timer for 15 minutes and just let your mind go wild and free there are no constraints

CHAPTER 6

CREATING YOUR CHAPTERS

You should have a small stack of cards in front of you with all your brainstorming questions, ideas, and thoughts.

You want to go through those and find the 7-10 biggest ideas or thoughts that will become your 7-10 chapters. I like to start with 10 and then throw out 2-3 that might not be as relevant or meaty as the others. Each big idea will be roughly 10 pages which will give you an 80 page book.

You want to pull out another 10 cards for each of your "chapter cards."

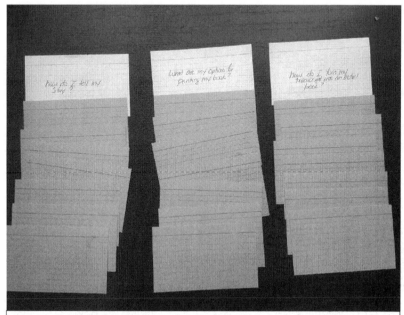

Grab 10 more blank index cards for each of your "chapter cards." You can see from this picture why those of us that are a little particular like colored index cards, because we can change the colors for the different uses.

Now, you want to brainstorm 7-10 burning questions, challenges, objections, stories, examples, points that you want to make in talking about each chapter card. You may find that some of these you already have from your first brainstorm.

You are still writing down 1 question or thought per index card. This time you are going to add to the back of the card a few prompts to help you remember what you want to talk about for that card.

For instance...

My chapter card is "Should you write a book" and my subchapter card is "Why should you write a book?" On the back of that card, I am going to bullet point the pieces that I want to talk about (hint: turn your card over from right to left instead of down to up so that you can read the cards)

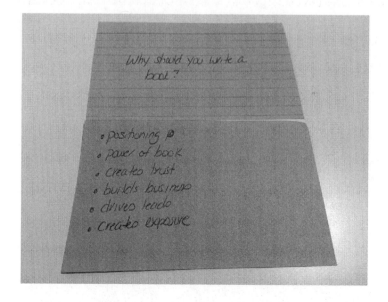

It's still best if you have these in a question format. You are not limited to 10 – continue to brainstorm as many as you can think of.

Hints for Burning Questions

Throughout this process, the more you can be speaking from your prospect's mind (and not your own) the easier these questions will be. There are no silly questions and nothing too small to ask.

Go back to what you put together in Chapter 3...

- What are your prospect's hidden secret desires that you can address here?
- What is keeping them awake at night?
- What do they really want to know?
- What is of REAL interest to them (not to you)?
- What are their real and imagined problems they are facing?

Let's Look at Example Chapter Cards and Ideas from Our Previous Examples

Example for a dentist whose chapter card is: "How do I prevent cavities?"

- Why do I always have cavities?
  - PH balances
  - Bacteria
  - Flossing vs. brushing
- Does it really "run in my family"?
  - Not genetic
  - Transfer of bacteria
  - Start as kids
- Why is fluoride important? Who should get it?
  - Teeth didn't change at 16
  - Still works today
  - Benefits
- How can sealants help?
  - Covers & protects the tooth
  - Not just for kids
  - Protect today or replace tomorrow
- How can power toothbrushes help?
- How do I prevent cavities in my kids?
- What's the difference between a crown and an implant?

Example for a real estate agent whose chapter card is: "What do I need to know as a first time home buyer?"

- What is a preapproval letter and do I need one?
    - Contact mortgage broker or bank
    - Credit check
    - Debt to credit ratio
- What additional fees are there on top of the purchase price?
    - Commissions
    - Closing costs
    - Hidden moving fees
- What does it cost to use a real estate agent?
    - How agents are paid
    - Who pays the agent
    - Paid at closing
- How long will the process take?
- What can I really afford?
- Should I rent or buy?

While these questions may seem mundane, or we start to think that everyone already knows this, to your prospect who is knee deep in their problems, this is all new information that they didn't know. We are so close to it that we assume that everyone knows the answers.

My Cards are Complete

Whoo hoo! Congratulations, the hardest part of this process is now finished ☺

Now, I want you to go through your cards and organize your thoughts inside of each chapter and then organize your chapters so that they are in the order that you want them.

You should finish with something that looks like this…

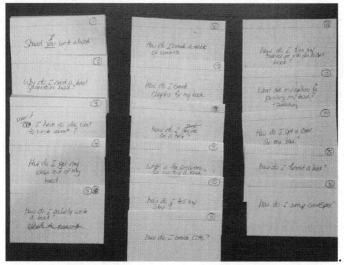

CHAPTER 7

HOW TO CREATE A TABLE OF CONTENTS THAT ENGAGES READERS

Now that you have your cards in the order that you believe that they will go in your book – remember you are still not tied to anything – you can actually create your table of contents before we even get to 'writing your book.'

I find myself changing the order of my chapters daily until my book is done. (For instance, you will see in my example cards that Chapters 6 and 7 were flip flopped in the final book.) But creating my table of contents helps me organize the flow of the book in my head and on paper. This is why we use index cards – because it's easy to change their order up.

In the upper right hand corner, I put the chapter number so that I can keep all my cards straight.

Let's talk about your table of contents – this shouldn't be an afterthought. After your title (which we haven't determined yet on purpose) and your table of contents are the most important parts of your book.

See, if we can't entice people to open our book, it won't matter what we write inside the book. Your table of contents needs to entice your reader to continue through your book.

We have briefly talked about entering the conversation that is already happening in the minds of your prospects, and you will see that comes out in your table of contents.

I had you write your index cards with questions that your prospects would ask, and now we are going to use those questions to create our table of contents. This way when the prospects skims through your table of contents they are reading the questions that they are thinking. In their minds (even if they never read the book) you are answering their biggest questions.

Plus, Amazon has this little feature called Look Inside, which allows browsers to view the first pages of your book before they buy. We will be using this feature to our benefit in two ways – the first is with our table of contents.

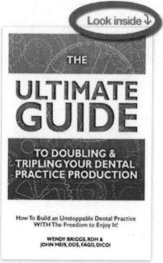

Example of a table of contents in the form of questions for a book on hiring super-stars;

CONTENTS

If you were looking for help in hiring, you've likely had bad experiences hiring, you've likely Googled everything under the

sun, but most of us are never trained in recruiting, interviewing, and hiring.

So each of those chapter questions was picked purposely.

"What if Everything You've Ever Learned about Hiring Employees is Wrong?" – this is picked as the first chapter on purpose. It piques the prospect's interest and states that what they are about to read is counterintuitive to what they have heard in the past.

"Why the Game is Rigged Against You" is meant to subconsciously arouse interest in the fact that hiring is actually a game and that you aren't set up to win the game.

"Why is it so Difficult to Hire Good People?" - this is a thought that goes through everyone's mind when they are interviewing unqualified person after person.

"Interview Questions that Really Work" – is another way of saying that the interview questions that you are currently using, don't work. And inside this book (the author) has interview questions that will actually work for you.

Compare that table of contents to most that you see…

CONTENTS

CHAPTER 8

HOW TO CREATE AN ATTENTION-GETTING TITLE

At this point, we are ready to create our title. I purposely wait to create the title so that you don't box your mind into a topic, idea or path by starting with your title. **The most powerful titles come AFTER you have a clear idea of what you will be talking about**.

We have now thought about our prospect, who they are; we have spent some time thinking about what they are thinking about, what they worry about, what answers they are seeking.

A good title won't make a good book, but a not-so-good title can definitely prevent your book from serving its purpose.

Our book is meant to be a marketing asset for our business so the last thing we want is a 'catchy' or 'cute' title that you might find on a best-selling fiction book. As a marketing asset, you want to treat your title like you would treat the headline of an ad.

The goal of our title is to:

- Have your reader understanding your book and its goals (what will they get from reading your book?)
- Make a promise or benefit to the reader
- Target a specific audience
- Offer solution to a specific problem
- Pique the curiosity of the reader

We also have the ability to use a subtitle to help us clarify our title and provide a longer explanation of the benefits held within our book. Your subtitle should be speaking to the desired outcomes and the big win that they are seeking.

When I first started working with a company, and I explained that I wanted to create a lead generation book to sell their coaching services, they told me that they had a book.

I asked for a copy so we could use it for marketing purposes. I was shocked with what they handed me: The X Factor … Building Your Dental Dream Team

So I went into their Createspace account to see how many copies of the book were sold. I wasn't surprised to find out that in the 2 years

that the book was out there, it had sold 23 copies.

I immediately went and changed the title of the book to call out to the target prospect, attract their attention and motivate a response. The book was rereleased under its new title: The Insider's Guide to Hiring a World-Class Dental Team... A Revolutionary Approach to Recruiting, Hiring, Training and Retaining World-Class Dental Professionals.

In the next 2 years, with no marketing, no other changes, just a title change, this book sold 123 copies. **Your title matters – your**

words matter.

I will warn you that once you publish this book, the title is the only thing that can not be easily changed. It's not impossible – you will need to retire the book under the old name and release a new book under the new name.

The job of your title is to get your reader to open the cover and start reading your book. They won't do that if they don't think the book is for them, or they don't know what they will get from giving their time to reading your book.

The time you take to determine your title is very well spent. When I teach this in the accelerated book writing workshop, we spend time first brainstorming the title and then bouncing the ideas off of the group. I guarantee you that every participant rarely ends up using their first title.

Easy Title Creation Templates

I suggest that you use these title creation

templates to brainstorm titles for your book. Start by filling in the blanks for each one and then choose the best one for you...

How to _____

A Simple Method for _____

How to Solve _____ Once and for All!

The Ultimate Guide to _____

The Step-By-Step Formula for _____

The Truth About ____ That ____ Doesn't Want You to Know

Insider Secrets About _____

A Simple Technique for _____

The Dirty Little Secret About _____

7 Secrets Your Competitors Don't Want You to Know About _____

Why Almost Every Expert is Wrong About _____

The No-Lose Way to _____

How to Quickly and Easily _____

The A-B-C Formula for _____

The Shocking Truth About _____

The Correct Way to _____

An Easy Cure For the _____

The ONLY Type of _____ You Should Ever Use

The FOOLPROOF Way to _____

The Art of _____

Confessions of _____

The End of _____

Download the Title Creation Worksheet for FREE

All of the worksheets mentioned in this book are available for FREE to readers at:
www.DarcyJuarez.com/freetoolkit

Make sure that you are calling out your audience. That it's clear in your title who you are talking to. Prospects want to feel like you are talking directly to them.

Example Titles from Other Students

-   The Ultimate Guide to Doubling & Tripling Your Dental Practice Production (How to Build an Unstoppable Dentist Practice With the Freedom to Enjoy It!)

-   The Business of Dental Hygiene (How to Create a Hygiene Driven Practice)

-   Behind the Steam Curtain (Powerful Secrets that your Local Dry Cleaner Won't Tell You)

-   How to Build Your Retirement Dream (Building a Million Dollar Retirement is Easier Than you Think When You Use the Right Tools)

-   How to Get More Customers and Make More Money (The Fastest Ways to Bring in More Customers, Revenue, and Profits for Your Business)

- I Just Want to Know it Will be OK (How to Build Your Retirement Portfolio to Ensure Peace of Mind)

Once you have your title, you will want to Google it and check on Amazon that your title is not already in use ☺

CHAPTER 9

THE STRESS-FREE PROCESS FOR *WRITING* YOUR BOOK

Most of us can talk faster than we can write. We can express ourselves verbally better than we can in print – so we will be using this to our advantage.

You will *talk* out your book, and then once you have the book verbalized, you can choose to finish the book yourself or at this point, you can hire outside help to help you finish the book.

No one can write what's in your head until you can get it out of your head. That's the biggest mistake that people make. They think that if they hire someone to write their book they won't have to do any work. But the truth is all the information, knowledge and expertise is locked in your head.

So let's grab your cards and you will want to ask a friend to help you by interviewing you. I suggest that it not be someone who is already close to your business (so not your spouse.) You want someone who won't connect any dots that you leave open, who can tell you when something is confusing.

Your Partner in Crime

Their job will be to read your question cards to you and let you answer the questions. You want them to ask you to clarify things that seem confusing, or where they don't feel like they have enough information.

While it may seem frustrating at the start, their clarifying questions and confusion will help you to create a better book. We are so close to our own businesses and our information that we don't always realize when we are confusing. We make assumptions that others already know a lot of information, but when we go back and we explain, even the simplest of ideas, our prospects feel safe and secure. They feel like we understand them.

Everyone asks, *"Do I have to have someone interview me? Can't I just record myself answering the questions?"* I have found that it is much easier to record anything when you are talking to another human being vs. talking directly to a computer screen.

There is something about seeing someone else's face, seeing their reactions, when they get excited about something, when the light bulbs go off, when they learn something new. That doesn't happen when you are having a one-sided conversation with an audio recorder.

When we are not talking to another person, we tend to shortcut our answers and we may not fully explain an idea or topic. It also has a calming effect and allows you to talk naturally and in a conversation, all of which come out and make for a better book.

You do want to make sure that you are in the same room for your interview. This can work over the phone, but you are not able to see their face as you are doing it.

Recording Your Interview

Now that you have your cards, you have someone to interview you, you will need a way to record the interview.

Like everything in technology, this becomes easier every year – because there is an app for that.

In the end, you just need a way to get an MP3 recording of your interview. Here are the 3 easiest ways that I suggest. You are free to use any way that you are comfortable with.

1. Use the Rev.com transcription app. Rev.com is one of the transcription services that I recommend for quick and

easy transcriptions. Using their app saves a step and allows you to send your audio file immediately to a transcriptionist. I make no money if you use their services – and there could be others that work the same or better – this is just one that I have found to be easy (and I believe that they give you $10 off your first transcription.)

2. A portable audio recorder or the audio recorder on your phone. If you have a portable audio recorder, these work great, they allow you to immediately download the MP3 file after your interview. The only reason I caution recording on your phone is that your chances of running out of storage space increases. The last thing you want is to have the recording stop when you are halfway way through your interview.

3. FreeConferenceCall.com allows you to set up a free conference line (if you are doing this as a phone interview) or an online meeting if you are doing this as an in-person interview.

The key is not to overcomplicate this from a technical standpoint. Your end goal is to have an MP3 file that you can send to a transcription service.

The Interview

I had you write your cards in question format so that this part of the process would be more natural and extract the most amount of information from you as possible – thus making the content of your book better.

** Make sure you press record ***

Then your interviewer is going to pick up your first chapter card and say *"Chapter 1"* and then read your question. You want to say that out loud on the recording so that your transcription picks it up. This will make the editing of your book move faster. It will be easy to see where your chapters start and stop.

They will then move on to your first subchapter card and read that question. Since they are sitting in front of you, they have the question facing them and the bullet points that you wrote on the back side are not easily readable by you ☺

It's very natural for us to answer questions. Don't worry about the fact that we are creating a book from this; simply talk to your interviewer like you would a prospect. Help them to understand you, what you do, your expertise and, most importantly, how you can help them. Share with them your knowledge and expertise.

The interviewer wants to let you finish your thoughts before asking any clarifying questions – this will prevent 'talking over' which is difficult to transcribe.

Good clarifying questions include…

- Tell me more about that.
- That didn't seem clear.
- Why did you do it that way?
- How exactly did you do that?
- What is the purpose of that?
- How exactly would I do that?
- What is my first step?

- What's the first thing I should do?
- Can you give me an example of that?

Your job as the interviewee is to relax. I would have a bottle of water nearby – it's more difficult than we think to talk for a few hours without taking a sip of water.

Remember, it's better to over explain something, it's easier to remove things from your book than it is to try and come up with more. Go ahead and say everything that you can think of on the topic.

Give examples whenever possible. If you have stories that you can tell to highlight your ideas, tell them. These all help the reader bond to you.

Remember, this is not your final version. This is just us getting that knowledge and expertise out of your head and onto the paper without you having to actually write a single word.

2-4 hours of recording should give you

80-150 pages of content.

Turning Your Interview Into Words on Paper

Now that you have finished your interview, if you recorded it using the Rev.com app, it's simply a click of the button to send that to be transcribed.

If you have an MP3 recording of your interview, either from your phone, a recorder, or from a conference line, you will want to upload it to a transcription service.

The reason that I recommend Rev.com is for their 12-hour turnaround. So I can spend the afternoon recording and then send my audio file to transcription overnight and have it in my in-box in the morning – so that I can continue working.

You can also use Transcribeme.com (personally I think their transcriptions are a little better, but they take a little longer and cost a little more), Temi.com (this is a new service that I haven't used yet), or tigerfish.com (who promises 2-hour turnaround – I haven't used them either.)

Congratulations! You have the first draft of your book done.

The hardest part is finished ... now we just have to clean it up, make it look 'pretty' and publish it.

Download my Step-by-Step Instructions for Recording Your Interview Using Freeconferencecall.com

All of the worksheets mentioned in this book are available for FREE to readers at:

www.DarcyJuarez.com/freetoolkit

CHAPTER 10

TELLING YOUR STORY

Many people fret over the "about the author" page. Personally, I like to incorporate your story into the first few chapters of the book. Unlike fiction books, you are an integral part of why someone will want to read this book.

So taking a little time to think over how you write this will go a long way. Your prospects need to feel like they know you, we are all looking for people that we connect with and this part of your book is how you will initiate that contact with your prospects.

We all have a back story, how we came to be who we are, why we are doing what we are doing, why we believe what we believe, who we advocate for, and, most importantly, why we are doing what we are doing.

This is your mythology, your legend, your lifestory summarized with the points that will matter to your prospects. That's a key piece – *the points that will matter to your prospects.* You want to think about your life history and determine which pieces will matter to your prospects and which won't be as relevant.

This can be difficult, because we don't always know what will connect with each individual person. It's why we might drop the name of the college we attended into our story – but not make a big deal out of it. For someone who attended the same school as you, this is a connection point and for those that didn't, it's a piece that they will pass over.

Your story should be told over and over again as a part of your marketing. We don't want a boring CV or resume-driven "about the author" story. Instead, we want to tell this as a story, where the prospect can see themselves inside the story. Where they connect to you for the little pieces that make you human.

To help you think about this, here is a list of potential aspects for your story. Brainstorm through the list, listing as many things as you can for yourself, and then we will weave these into a story you can use. I am always amazed at the stories that come out from this exercise at the accelerated book writing workshop. We start day 1 with everyone introducing themselves, and we start day 2 with everyone reading their stories. Many times you wouldn't be able to connect the two together unless you were sitting there.

Potential Aspects for Your Story

- The enemies you battle (idiot ad agencies and big dumb companies, lazy, incompetent people)

- What makes you different (former Iowa prison guard)
- Physical description
- Birthplace
- Childhood events and influences (stuttering, poor parents, no education)
- Education
- Family
- Ambitions
- Adventures
- Successes
- Failures (people don't believe people who have never failed)
- Core Belief
- Pathological behaviors
- Greatest talents or skills
- Incompetencies
- Likes / dislikes
- Pet peeves
- Eccentricities
- Politics
- Religion
- Hobbies and interests
- Significant life events
- Things people will be curious about...
- Things people will be amazed by ...
- Things people will envy / desire ...

Then you want to simply tell it as a story that will connect to your prospects. Most importantly **why** are you talking to them on the topic that you are talking to them on?

Here is an example template that I wrote for an information marketer who helps companies hire super-star employees. It was important that we bring to light and connect him to small business owners. You will notice a line in here stating that *"I wrote this book specifically for..."*

My name is xxxxxxx, and I have spent the better part of my adult life helping entrepreneurs and small business owners hire super-stars in their respective businesses. And I can tell you that, while it's not easy, it is something you can do and I'll show you how.

I have worked with large corporations, Fortune 500 companies, and the local mom-and-pop bakery and every single business regardless of its size, location, or personnel struggle with hiring the 'right' people. I wrote this book specifically for the entrepreneur and small business owner (the local dentist, attorney, or bakery) because I watched my dad struggle for so many years to find good help in his small business.

In fact, I watched my dad's disappointment with the poor performance that came from his team, even management-level people. I remember [fill in with memories of your dad struggling]

If you're like my dad, and are currently struggling with [list struggles], People say they can do the job but then they don't perform. Attitudes affect the whole culture and team. Create turnover. Make simple costly mistakes. Don't show up on time. Lose business simply in the way they speak with potential clients, customers, patients. Are not committed or engaged.

I'm here to show you that there is a better way!

We talked about the struggles that we knew that they had, we are talking directly to them and letting them know that this book is written specifically for them. We shed light on his background and history.

Here is a version that I wrote for me. I use this story when I am teaching marketing (so you will see a very heavy focus on marketing-related connections.)

Hi, my name is Darcy Juarez, and I haven't always been an entrepreneur, and I can tell you that being an entrepreneur didn't come easy. I grew up, like many, the oldest child of middle-class parents who were determined to do better financially than their parents did and provide their children with a 'good life.' My mom was an in-home daycare provider (she has patience that I will never have!) and my dad worked for the Chicago Public School system for 39 years and retired with a pension – so you can imagine how many times I heard from my grandmother (his mother) "Why can't you just stay with one job? How will you ever have security in your life?"

I am sure she rolls over in her grave every time I change my "job." But the fact is, today there is no such thing as security from a "job." But I found security ... it's in having the skills and knowledge to be able to create customers, generate cash, and keep customers buying more. When you have those 2 skills you have created your own security!

But I didn't start out that way ... I knew I was lucky enough to receive a full-ride Division 1 scholarship to play volleyball – but I didn't know what I wanted to do after that.

I graduated with a degree in Parks and Rec (yes, it is a real degree ☺) and my first job was with Arthur Andersen... a job using my recreation degree where I got to run around in sweatpants while everyone else had to wear business suits, but

I quickly (well I guess if you call 4 years quickly) learned that I couldn't stand all the red tape. The ideas and plans that I created in my first year still hadn't come to fruition by the time I left. But I loved going to work in sweatpants!

So I moved on to manage a small family run physical therapy center. The only 'medical knowledge' I had was what I experienced going through 2 surgeries after College. But I was willing to learn (which is a whole other topic for another book on hiring), and within 2 years I had created enough systems and automation that I could do my 'job' in just 4 hours ... I had automated myself out of a job!

At that time, a friend of mine was looking for help with a business that he was starting and just like physical therapy, I knew nothing about running a business but quickly learned that if we didn't make customers appear, there wasn't going to be enough money to go around. And just like that, I engrossed myself in learning everything I could about marketing and sales, and we doubled the profits in that business year after year for a good 4 years before creating additional business, one of which I am still involved with today. And that entrepreneurial bug was born – I LOVED that if I had an idea, I could implement it today and see results today! It wasn't long before I had people wanting me to teach them the "tricks" I was using to have such success ... Which is why I wrote this book for all the entrepreneurs who are looking to create a steady stream of customers who will pay, stay and refer.

Now it's your turn. This isn't a novel in and of itself. You only need a few paragraphs to allow your prospects a chance to connect with you.

CHAPTER 11

CREATING YOUR CALL TO ACTIONS

We call this a lead generation book, because its purpose is to drive leads to our business and convert those leads into customers.

This means that we need to include a call to action or multiple calls to action telling the reader what they should do next.

You have a few options and ways to accomplish this. If this is your first book, I suggest that you only worry about having a call to action (CTA) at the end and possibly at the front of your book. Don't worry about making it complicated or delaying the release of your book, because you don't have a CTA ready to go.

Let's start with the simple CTA for your first book. This will be on the last page of your book and will tell your reader what you want them to do next.

The template for this is simple...

Now that you know x [summary of the big idea of your book], here's what you should do next.

So that might look like this if I am a Realtor...

Now that you know the ins and outs of buying your first home, you can choose a real estate agent who will be your partner and you will soon be waking up in the home of your dreams. If I can help you find your home ...

It might look like this if I was a marketing consultant...

Now that you know 7 different ways to find new clients, you can confidently take action and have a steady stream of clients calling you. If I can help you ...

We can't assume that our prospects will know what to do next. In the marketing world, we talk about creating call to actions that a 10-year-old can follow. You wouldn't skip steps when asking a child to do a task (because they take you literally.) You want to do the same when you are giving instructions to your prospect.

You want to have explicit instructions on what to do next.

This is an example from the hiring book...

If you are like most people, I am guessing that you LOVE what you have read here, you believe that if you could know this information about potential hires (or even your current employees) it would be beyond beneficial, but aren't sure HOW to go about this or are not sure if this can really tell you everything I say it can.

I want to offer you my "Try It Before You Buy It" Risk-Free Offer. I want you to take the profile, or have one of your key employees (someone who you know well) take this 15-min. profile. Then jump on the phone with me for a 30-min. debrief, and if in those 30 minutes I don't tell you something you didn't know about your key employee or something no one knows about you, then not only will I give you your money back, I will also donate an additional $100 to the charity of your choice.

Go to www.XXXXXXX.com for this Risk-Free opportunity.

Advanced Call To Actions at the Beginning and End of Your Book

Earlier, I mentioned that we would use the "Look Inside" feature from Amazon. The first place was for our table of contents and the second place is here, for your call to actions.

It's possible to drive leads to your business without anyone ever purchasing your book. It requires intentional placement of a CTA at the beginning of your book, which can appear when someone uses the "Look Inside" feature.

You will notice that at the beginning of this book, I have strategically placed a CTA before the book even starts to be able to get the book as an audio, as well as to get the toolkit that I reference throughout the book.

DOWNLOAD THE AUDIOBOOK AND TOOLKIT (INCLUDING ALL THE WORKSHEETS) FOR FREE!

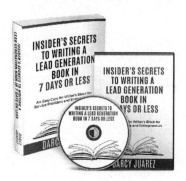

READ THIS FIRST

Just to say thanks for reading my book, I would like to give you the audiobook version PLUS the accompanying toolkit (which includes all the templates and worksheets) absolutely FREE.

Go to www.DarcyJuarez.com/freeaudiobook

This allows people who are interested and may not have even purchased the book to request more information from me, and for me to be able to follow up with those interested.

You can use a CTA to go straight to a call with you, like I did in this example:

The Most Incredible Free Gift Ever....

Claim Your $2,998 Dental Practice Growth Gift

Valid for 1 60-minute Practice Analysis Amplifier. The Team Training Institute will analyze your current practice and provide you with a roadmap to implement all 5 key areas of growth in your practice.

To CLAIM Your Gift:
www.HowToDoubleProduction.com/freegift

You can get really advanced and create a free membership site where people can register to access more information on your topic or services:

11 Habits of Highly Successful Dentists

Free Resources Just For Book Readers!

Because this topic is so important to the Dental Community and because everyone learns differently, we have created a special area for readers of the 11 Habits of Highly Successful Dentists.

The great news is access to this area is completely free.

You can register and receive free access at...

www.11Habits.com/free

Here's what you will find when you register for your free access...

* All of the downloadable resources mentioned throughout the book.

* 3 advanced video trainings on the 11 Secrets of Highly Successful Dentists

* BONUS Audio Training: How to Instantly Add $20,000 to your practice by Conducting Successful Morning Huddles!

* BONUS Video Training: What Got You To Where You Are Today Won't Get You To Where You Want To Go Tomorrow

Simply register to receive free access at:
www.11Habits.com/free

Advanced Call to Actions Throughout Your Book

In addition to CTAs at the beginning and end of your book, you have the ability to pepper specific CTAs throughout your chapters. What I like to use, is the ability to download a PDF or infographic related to the information that you just provided in that chapter.

This is an example for readers to be able to download a PDF for a brochure that was just explained in the chapter:

To download a FREE copy of this brochure and access my FREE training on how this one tool accounts for 90% of my case acceptance and how I can do it all in 90 seconds of less go to:

www. ▮▮▮▮▮▮▮▮▮▮ .com/risk-assessment-brochure

This is an example to download templates

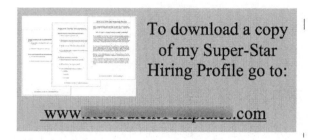

To download a copy
of my Super-Star
Hiring Profile go to:

www._____.com

Remember, you can always come back and add more CTAs in Versions 2 and above. Version 1 of your book only needs one call to action.

CHAPTER 12

TURNING YOUR TRANSCIPT INTO YOUR BOOK

Now that you have your transcription, you will want to go through under two different goals. Your first pass through will be for content.

I start out by reading my transcript out loud. We 'wrote' this by talking, and so it will come more naturally if you continue the conversation. While reading the transcript, you want to note any places where you think you need to come back and add content, clarify anything, or where you feel there are gaps in the content.

During this same pass through, I am adding in the transitions for my chapters.

Transitions are simply a sentence or two that bridges the reader from one chapter to the next.

The template for the beginning of the chapter is *to tell them what you are going to tell them.* And you can end each chapter by *recapping what they learned in the chapter.*

So if I was a Realtor with a chapter on "The costs associated with buying a home," it might look like this...

First sentence of the chapter:

"In this chapter we are going to look at the 3 major costs associated with buying a home and, more importantly, how you can ensure that these costs are kept to a minimum."

Last sentence of the chapter:

"Now that you have a handle on the 3 biggest costs associated with purchasing a home, let's take a look at how you can secure the financing and be sure that you are receiving the best rates."

Next, I want to make sure that I have added my call to actions into the transcript (if I haven't done this already.)

With my transitions and call to actions in place and any new content added, I will give it one more read through, and I will add in subheads in larger chapters to help breakup the copy and keep the reader moving.

The Second Step to Turn Your Transcript into a Book

At this point, you should have a book that flows from a content standpoint. Now is when you can outsource or hire someone to help you. You have gotten all your knowledge and expertise out of your head, you have read through the transcript to ensure that you agree with everything and all that is left is to clean it up, correct any grammar and punctuation and lay this out in a book format.

Most people don't realize that even if you hired someone to write the book for you, you are still going to have to read through the final copy to ensure they have represented you and your thoughts, ideas, and expertise correctly.

But you don't have to be the one to spend the time cleaning up your transcript ☺

If you are outsourcing this, you may be looking for 2 different people to help you.

1. A ghostwriter can take your transcript and massage your transitions and content to help it flow better. They may or may not take this all the way through an "editing" phase.

2. An editor will only be reading to correct grammar and punctuation, they will not likely help you with flow.

Both can be very helpful and well worth the few hundred dollars you may pay them.

The best place to find this help is on Upwork (upwork.com) where you can post for project-related jobs, pick your price range and then ultimately choose a freelancer to help you. For an editor, I usually pay $1/page.

Section 3

Printing and Publishing Your Book

Congratulations, you have finished the most difficult part of this process – writing your book! Now you are ready to tackle the confusing part of actually publishing your book. As we talked about earlier, self-publishing is the best route to go for your lead generation book because our goal is to promote our celebrity, authority and expertise to our audience. As the title self-publishing says, this will require you to do the publishing. In this section, I will break down the options and walk you through the steps to have your book on Amazon within a few days.

CHAPTER 13

CREATING YOUR ATTENTION-GETTING COVER

In Chapter 8, you created the title for your book, and in this chapter we get to turn that title into an attention-getting cover. This is the part that for most really solidifies the fact that you have written a book.

It's my favorite part of our Accelerated Book Writing Workshops – watching the faces of the participants light up with joy, feeling so proud of what they accomplished – when I hand them a copy of their book covers. I always suggest that they keep that mock-up copy with them to remind them that the work that they are putting in will be paying off in spades for years to come.

I can't wait to see that for you!

The Goal of Your Book Cover

The goal of your cover is to stand out and magnetically attract <u>your</u> prospect. It's not to win any design awards.

The saying "never judge a book by its cover" is completely false – your book is absolutely being judged by its cover.

Here are a few things you want to think about when designing your book cover:

- **A large title** that is easily readable in a thumbnail image. Think about this, in pictures and marketing, we rarely have much more than a thumbnail image size available – if they can't clearly read your title, why would they be interested in your book?

- **The title in the upper third** of the book. The human eye works from top to bottom when skimming and focuses on the top of any page. The same is true for your book cover. Keep the title to the top third of the book – don't use this for your name or images. Make sure the most important thing – the title – is the emphasis of the book

- **Pictures that support your message.** I hate to break it to you, but people don't care about your photo – they care about themselves. So if you are using photos or images, make sure that they are enhancing your message. Make sure that your images are professional and high-resolution so that they will print well. You don't want to use clipart that will make your book appear "cheap." Make sure that you have purchased the rights to use any images used on your book covers – don't just download images from Google.

This is a place that I wouldn't skimp. I have used Fiverr.com to see if I could get a good book cover for $5, and I've found that I can get decent covers. But the covers that have blown me away have always been created by a graphic designer.

If you don't have a graphic designer, you can post the job on Upwork. I have also found that if you are a part of Facebook groups, this is a great place to ask if anyone recommends a graphic designer for a freelance project.

There is an online design site called 99designs where you pay a fee to have graphic designers create images and compete to win the bid. You then get to choose from the designs submitted and the designer who wins is paid through the site. This is great if you want to see a variety of designs to choose from.

Inside of CreateSpace, you have the opportunity to work with one of their designers to create your book cover.

Any of these options will work; you just need to determine which is best for you.

What is Needed for Your Book Cover?

Whoever designs your cover will need some basic information to complete your design:

Your book description: This is used on your back cover and when describing your book on Amazon. This is 150-250 words describing your book and why someone would want to read it.

The first sentence should grab the reader's attention and let them know immediately that the book is for them. This is written in the third person (while your book is best written in the first person.)

To make this easy, I like to use copy-written bullet points that provide the reader with quick snapshots of what's included in the book.

Your author bio: This is used on your back

cover as well as on Amazon. You can go through the story that you wrote in Chapter 10 and pull out the pieces that you want to use for this short bio.

This is roughly 250 words and demonstrates your authority and credibility on the topic. This could include the number of clients served, the number of years you have been in business, the products you have created, the number of countries using your advice, the hours you have spent learning your skills, your professional degrees, certifications you have earned, etc. *Why should the reader listen to you?*

Include pieces that will build your credibility or are interesting … family history in the business, interesting tidbits on how you got started, awards you have won, recognitions you've received, hobbies, etc. *Help the reader understand why they should spend time with you.*

Name-drop without name-dropping. If you have a well-known name to your readers to leverage, you want to do it in a way that doesn't sound off-putting or like you are just name-dropping to name-drop. For example, I might have a sentence like *"The woman who Dr. Woody Oakes calls the most popular hygiene trainer of our time."* That name will only be a big deal in that niche.

Mention your website, any other books written, how they can reach you in a very conversational way. *Find out more about [your name] at www.xxxx.com.*

Keep this to your most important pieces – as your bio grows, you can update your book cover.

Your headshot: It's totally up to you if you want to include your photo with your bio. For speed I will often leave that off. If you do include your photo, make sure it is high resolution so that it will print well.

Design brief: You will want to provide your designer with a design brief so that she can interpret your ideas and your vision into your design. The clearer you are, the better your design will be.

Conceptualize and communicate your vision. This is hard for just about anyone, which is one of the reasons that I encourage students to use a design that is all about the title (and not about the images).

Provide examples of what you do like. In our Accelerated Book Writing Workshops, the students are given a set of book cover designs that all have different looks and feels and ask to pick one that they like.

This way the designer has something to work with. You can do this by searching Amazon and picking out a handful of book covers that you gravitate towards.

Download a Copy of the Design Brief

we use with our designer along with all of the worksheets by going to:
www.darcyjuarez.com/freetoolkit

Your book cover measurements: Your designer will need to know the measurement for your book – which you will be able to get through CreateSpace – so that your front cover, back cover and spine all print correctly for your book.

CHAPTER 14

WHAT ARE MY OPTIONS TO PRINT AND PUBLISH MY BOOK?

One of the barriers to having your own book used to be the cost required to print books on small runs. Price breaks in printing don't usually happen until you are into the hundreds, if not thousands of copies.

Which is why you used to hear the nightmares from those who had written a book of the boxes and boxes that were taking up space in their garage or basement. And you can imagine the headache and costs when you wanted to change something in your book.

Thanks for the book giant Amazon, we now have CreateSpace, which is an Amazon company that allows for independent publishing and, more importantly, allows you to leverage their millions of clients for very inexpensive printing. With CreateSpace you are able to print copies of your book in lots as small as a few copies and all the way up to hundreds, all depending on what your needs are.

The printing is the main reason that I publish on CreateSpace, and a very nice little by-product is that your book can appear on Amazon (and who doesn't want to see themselves on Amazon? Think of how proud your mom will be!)

While our goal isn't to make money selling our book on Amazon, you will likely start receiving royalty checks from people who find your book on Amazon and buy it ☺

No one is going to be retiring with these royalty checks, but you might be able to go out for a nice dinner each year thanks to the royalty checks.

If Amazon isn't for you, you can find a local or internet printer and simply print your books up for use in your office, you don't have to actually publish your book.

You can also use print-on-demand services like;

- 48hrbooks.com
- Diggypod.com
- Ingramspark.com
- Thebookpatch.com

I don't think any will hold a candle to the convenience and pricing available with CreateSpace.

Since I use the books as lead generation tools, I am constantly ordering copies of the books for my businesses (so I only pay the wholesale cost) for as little as $2.00 a book. Now, there are no royalties on the wholesale prices, but I haven't found a printer that can print a book for that low of a cost. In fact, many times, the book costs me less than any brochure, pamphlet or marketing piece that the printer is printing for us.

In Chapter 16, I will walk you through everything you need to do to print and publish with CreateSpace.

CHAPTER 15

FORMATTING YOUR BOOK FOR EASY READING

When you are ready to lay out your book, I like to download the Word document template for my book size from CreateSpace.

Personally, I like the book size 6x9 or 5.5x8.5 as those are the most popular book sizes.

I have found that there are a few things that you can do to format your book for easy reading. After all, the goal of our book is to give our prospects a glimpse into our world – but they won't stay there for hours upon hours. So anything we can do to make this easy for them to consume, the better.

Keep paragraphs to 1-2 sentences: I keep my paragraphs to 1 thought. As soon as I find myself with a new thought or more than 2 sentences, I am looking for a natural break where I can start a new paragraph.

If readers start to skip ahead, it's usually to the next paragraph, so I make that easy for them to do.

Make it easy to read: This chapter started out as 3 pages.

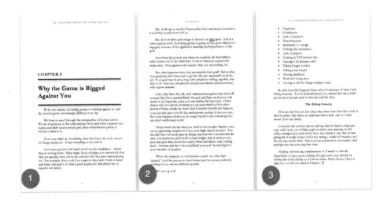

First, I increased the paragraph font from 12pt to 14pt, which is easier to read and will add some length to the book.

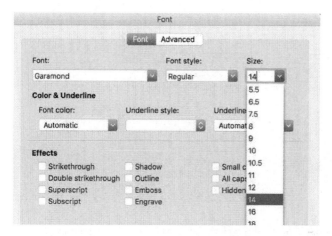

Then I increase the paragraph setting.

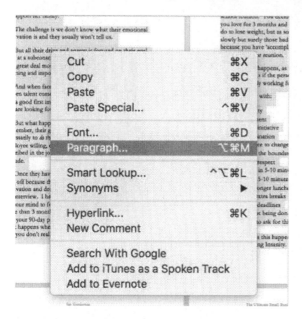

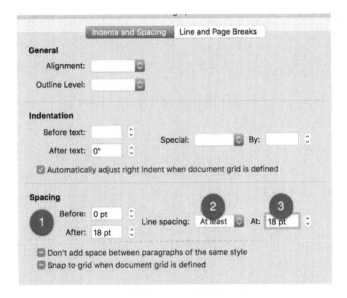

1. Increase the after from 12pt to 18pt
2. The line spacing from "single" to "at least"
3. From 12pt to 18pt

Just by doing these 2 things I make the book easier to read and have increased my chapter from 3 pages to 5 pages.

Add subheads: To break up your copy and make it easier to read.

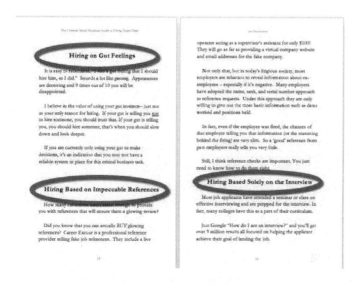

Start chapters on odd pages: When we are flipping through a book, our eyes naturally go to the right-hand side. Which is why I like to start all my chapters on right-hand-side pages. Which are the odd-pages in your setup.

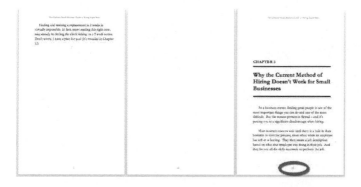

CHAPTER 16

A STEP-BY-STEP WALK-THROUGH TO SET UP CREATESPACE

The following is a walk-through of Createspace and is included as a document in the toolkit which you can download for free by going to www.darcyjuarez.com/freetoolkit.

Go to www.createspace.com and click on "sign up."

Complete your registration and create your account

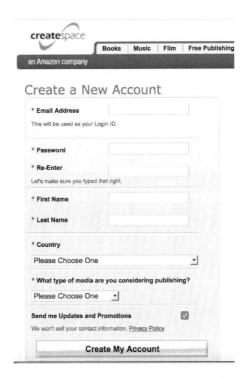

While creating your account, you will need to fill out tax information for any royalty checks. Yes, you will have people who find your book and buy your book through Amazon ☺. For speed, you may want to fill this out as an individual and go back with your business information at a later time (as you will need your tax Id and additional information.) CreateSpace won't let you get started if you don't fill out the tax information.

From the member dashboard – you want to "Add a New Title"

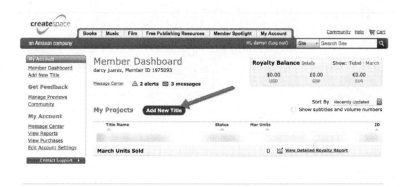

You want to name your project – I make mine the name of my book, choose "paperback" and then "Guided" setup process.

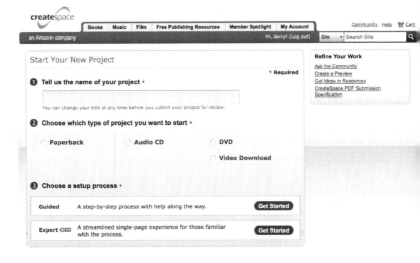

Fill in your title information. Your title, once saved, cannot change. But you can always retire the book and create a new one.

ISBN (or International Standard Book Numbers) are the 10-13 digit numbers created to intimidate us and make the publishing process more complicated. I know the first time I looked at this I went running scared!

The ISBN number allows bookstores and publishers to identify books – if there are 2 books with the same title, the ISBN allows them to easily identify which is which.

If you are publishing through CreateSpace and only intend on selling through Amazon, you can use the CreateSpace-assigned ISBN for free. This what I recommend for your lead generation book.

If you are publishing through any other printer, you will need to buy your own ISBN. ISBNs can be purchased through Bowker for $129 (you will need a different ISBN for each version of your book; paperback, audiobook, ebook.)

ISBN	
CreateSpace Assigned	We can assign an ISBN to your book at no charge. This cannot be changed once you saved your progress
Enter Your Own	If you have an ISBN for this book that you purchased from R.R. Bowker.

Choose your Physical Properties

1. Interior type – unless you are a graphic designer who needs to showcase color images, use black & white for your interior pages. This keeps your price per book extremely reasonable
2. Paper color – this is a personal choice
3. Trim size – I choose 6x9, the most popular size for paperback books
4. After choosing your trim size, you will be able to download the Word template. This template will make laying out your book simple and easy as all the margins have been set for you.

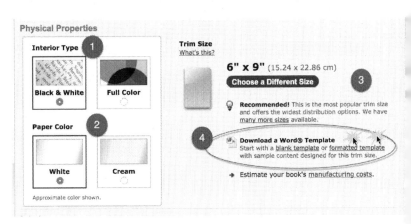

Your books interior: At this point, you need to upload a PDF of your interior files. You want to use the template you just downloaded, add the edited version of your book, and save as a PDF to upload. You can come back and reupload interior files at any time (meaning you can change anything inside of your book at any time.)

If you make changes after your book has been published, CreateSpace will take roughly 24 hours to approve the new material before it's available.

If you want to 'trick' the system, save the template you just downloaded as a PDF and upload that now so that the system will let you continue setting up your book. ** Just remember to come back and replace it with your real copy ☺

I leave the bleed set as "before the edge of the page."

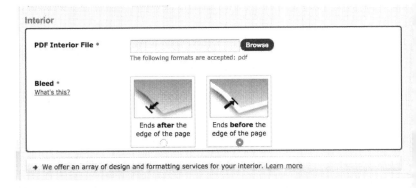

For your cover: Now is when you will upload the cover created by your designer; below, I have included the cheat sheet locations to provide for the designer so they can provide you with an accurate cover design. This template will leave the appropriate spaces for your ISBN and bar codes.

CHEAT SHEET LOCATIONS FOR YOUR COVER DESIGNS

Go to:

https://www.createspace.com/Products/Book/CoverPDF.jsp for the full instructions for designing your own cover. This may seem overwhelming and confusing, but most designers are familiar with these measurements.

Go to:

https://www.createspace.com/Help/Book/Artwork.do to calculate the measurements for your specific cover. You will need to know the number of pages for your book (to get an accurate spine size)

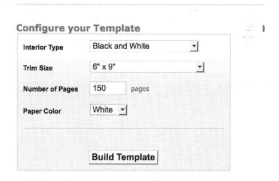

This will give you a downloadable template for your designer to lay out.

RETURN TO CREATESPACE SETUP

Choose your cover finish – this is a personal preference.

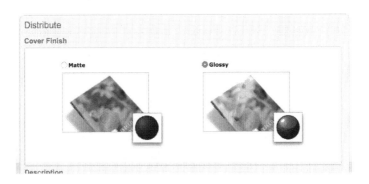

Description: Here is where you will insert the description you have written for your book

Description

Why Are We Working Harder and Making Less Money?

Description *
What's this?

Maximum 4000 characters - 4000 characters remaining
Advanced users can use limited HTML instead of plain text to style and
format their description

Category: You are able to choose the category where your book will reside. You want to get as granular as possible so that your book is better seen. For example, if I was writing a book targeted for dentists to grow their practices, I would choose Medical – Dentistry – Practice Management instead of leaving it in the general Medical category.

BISAC Category *
What's this?

➔ **Enter a BISAC code**

Juvenile Nonfiction >	Cardiology
Language Arts & Disciplines >	Caregiving
Law >	Chemotherapy
Literary Collections >	Chiropractic
Literary Criticism >	Clinical Chemistry
Mathematics >	Critical Care
Medical >	Dentistry >
Music >	Dermatology
Nature >	Diagnosis
Non-Classifiable >	Dictionaries & Terminology
Performing Arts >	Diet Therapy
Pets >	Diseases
Philosophy >	Drug Guides

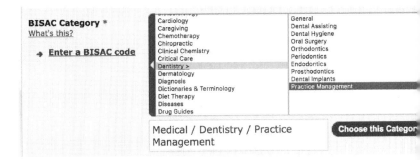

Adding Additional Information:

- You will want to click on the "add" for the author biography and insert the author bio that you wrote and choose your country of publication.

- You will want to add your keywords: Search keywords can help your title show up on both Amazon.com and search engines. Pick phrases that you think customers are likely to use when either searching for your title specifically or when shopping for products that may be similar in subject matter. You can add up to five keyword phrases separated by commas.

- Assuming that your content isn't restricted to 18 and over, you will leave

the "contains adult content" box
unchecked.

- The large print is for if your book is for
the visually impaired and includes print
at greater than 16pt.

Once you have saved everything, you can
move on to setting up your channels for
distribution. It's up to you if you want to use
the expanded distribution. For the purpose of
your lead generation book, you only need
Amazon.com.

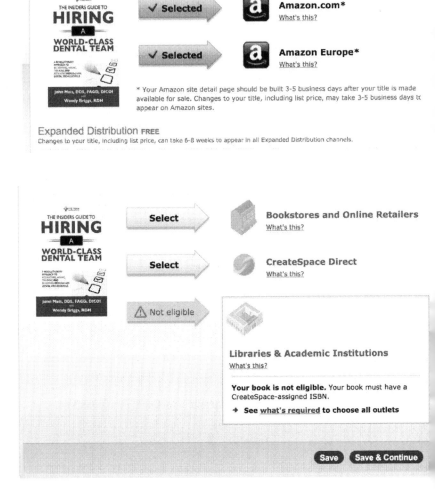

Pricing: Next, you will set up the pricing for your book on Amazon. I price my books reasonably – usually $14.95 but up to $19.99. Once you provide your USD Price, CreateSpace will auto-calculate and make suggestions for the other prices. You can adjust your prices at any time (another reason I don't suggest putting the price on your cover design.)

CONGRATULATIONS! Your book is now ready to publish on Amazon.com.

To complete the publishing process:

1. You will need to complete the interior review of your book.

2. After uploading the final version of your interior file, you will be asked if you wish to complete the interior review – choose yes.

3. CreateSpace will send you a message after they complete the review and you will be able to order 1 proof copy of your book.

4. Once you approve your proof book, it will take 2-4 business days for your book to appear on Amazon.com.

Ordering books for your own use:

The biggest reason for publishing your lead generation book on CreateSpace was to leverage their printing and pricing.

Once your book is approved, it will appear as "Available" from your member dashboard.

At this time, you can click on "order copies" and purchase as many copies as you would like, and you will pay the wholesale price (usually between $2-$3/copy.)

Which means that you can keep copies of your book in your office and hand out in place of business cards, brochures and less effective marketing materials that likely cost you more than your newly published book ☺

ABOUT THE AUTHOR

Darcy Juarez has spent the last 15 years creating some of the most successful product launches and marketing systems in the direct response and information marketing world. And the one thing that every one of those had in common is that their successful lead generation campaigns started with a book.

Five years ago, she started teaching her process for *writing* these lead generation books to a group of high implementers at the GKIC Peak Performer's meeting, and after seeing their success and the speed at which they could implement this system, started teaching this to other entrepreneurs.

Darcy has a unique ability to translate complex and daunting tasks (like writing a book) into simple and easy-to-use systems that anyone can follow. As an avid athlete growing up, time was always of the essence, and Darcy always finds the most efficient ways to operate, so it doesn't surprise anyone who knows her that she cracked the code on how to write a book in 7 days or less.

She has witnessed firsthand how many entrepreneurs are paralyzed by the fear of the unknown, by counterintuitive ideas, and by the fear of what others will think.

Which is why she wrote this book. To tackle all of this head on because she knows how important and necessary this incredibly valuable tool is for every entrepreneur ... and most people never get this done.

DOWNLOAD THE AUDIOBOOK AND TOOLKIT (INCLUDING ALL THE WORKSHEETS) FOR FREE!

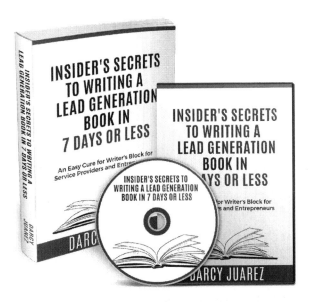

READ THIS FIRST

Just to say thanks for reading my book, I would like to give you the audiobook version PLUS the accompanying toolkit (which includes all the templates and worksheets) absolutely FREE.

Go to www.DarcyJuarez.com/freeaudiobook

Made in the USA
San Bernardino, CA
17 July 2020

75691891R00091